Fun Is A Feeling

ILLUMINATION ARTS
PUBLISHING COMPANY, INC.
BELLEVUE, WASHINGTON

To all of our feelings
and the vision they bring.

The Dr. Samuel G. Brooks Guild
for the Seattle Children's Hospital

gifts

_____

this book. Let the story help you
'Let the Fun Out'
Chara M. Curts
Cynthia Aldrich

Fun Is
A Feeling

Words by Chara M. Curtis

Illustrations by Cynthia Aldrich

Concept by Chara and Cynthia

I once met a man who had so much fun
I just had to ask him how it was done.
He juggled my question a moment or two,
Then he laughed, ''Fun or not…it's all up to you!

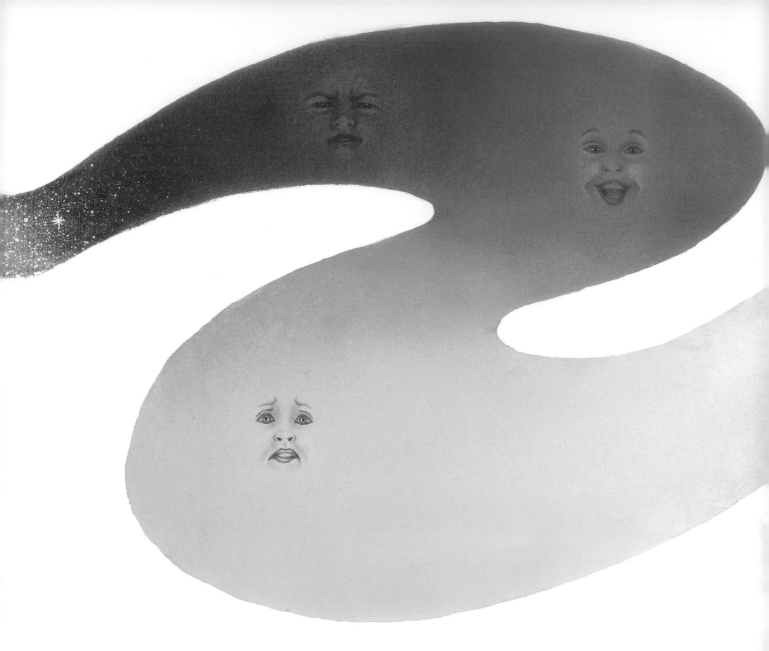

Fun isn't *something* or *somewhere* or *who;*
It's a feeling of joy that lives inside of you.
You can feel happy, or you can feel sad….
Joy comes from knowing no feeling is bad.

Treasure your feelings and treat them with care.
Pay close attention to the wisdom they share.
This is the way to become your best friend,
And then—you can have fun without end!

Fun can be found wherever you go,
But there's one more thing I think you should know.
Sometimes it hides, because fun LOVES to play,
And waits till you see things a different way.

Consider the courage of that little bug
Who jumped on your nose to give you a hug...
Or the soft, silken lace of a wondrous design
That a spider created as your valentine!

Feel the kiss of a raindrop, see the wink of a star—
Magic reminders of how loved you are.
Or picture yourself with a swashbuckling friend
Riding a whale to the Land of Pretend.

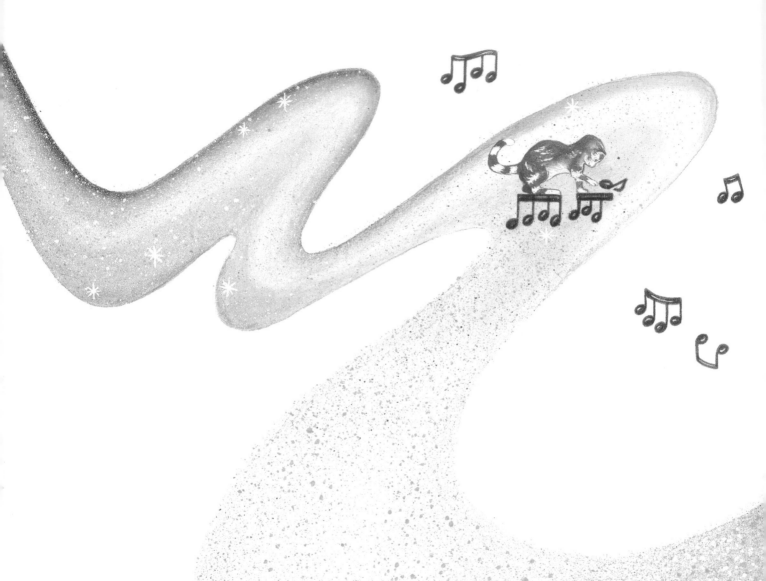

When you see things this way, you put joy in your heart.
And when your heart's full, you've done the first part.
The rest is so easy—what fun's all about—
Just open your heart…and LET YOUR FUN OUT!

Mermaids will spill from your bathwater spout
And glide to the sea on a rainbow of trout.
While sea lions slide from your slippery knees,
Porpoises balance on bubbles with ease.

It's all what you make it. It's all what you see.

Only YOU can create how you want it to be!

The next time you're bored, make a smile from your frown…

Just stand on your head, and you've turned it around!

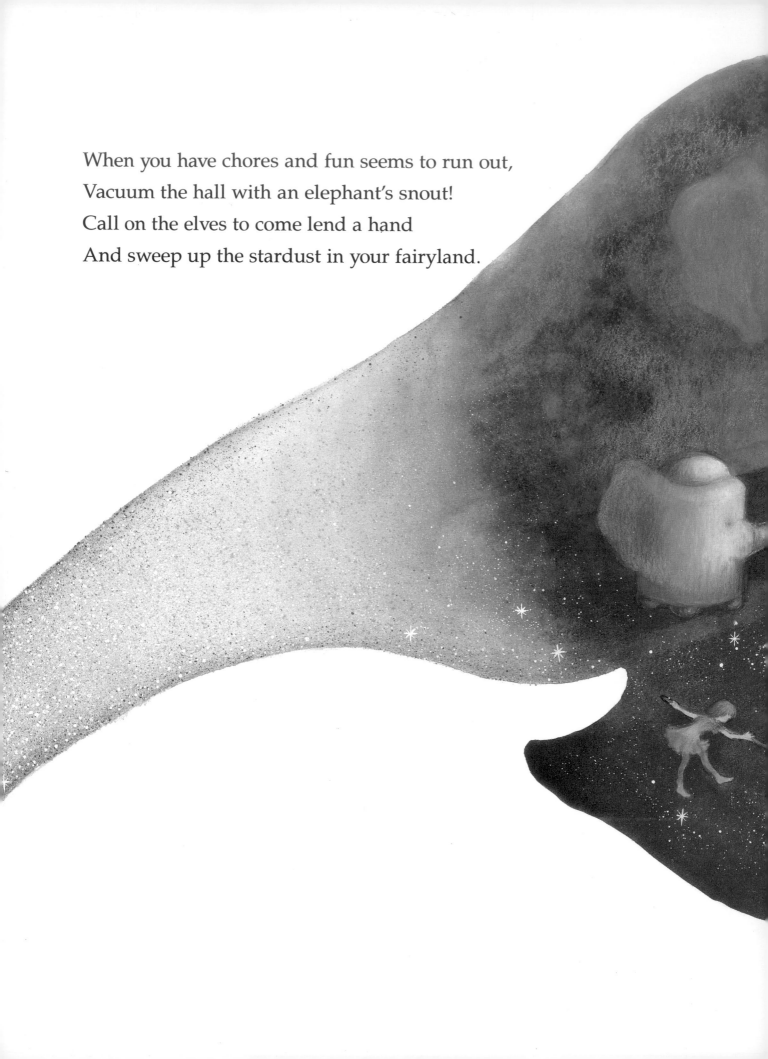

When you have chores and fun seems to run out,
Vacuum the hall with an elephant's snout!
Call on the elves to come lend a hand
And sweep up the stardust in your fairyland.

Not everyone's notion of fun is the same.
Some like it wild and some like it tame.
Some like the opera, some like the zoo,
And sometimes pretending is all you can do.

I'm so glad you've asked me about having fun—
A valuable question, when all's said and done—
For you make the world a more beautiful place
With the light in your eyes and the grin on your face.

You're so important that each time you smile
The joy that you feel travels mile after mile.
It crosses the mountains and swims through the seas.
It flies through the air and tickles the trees!

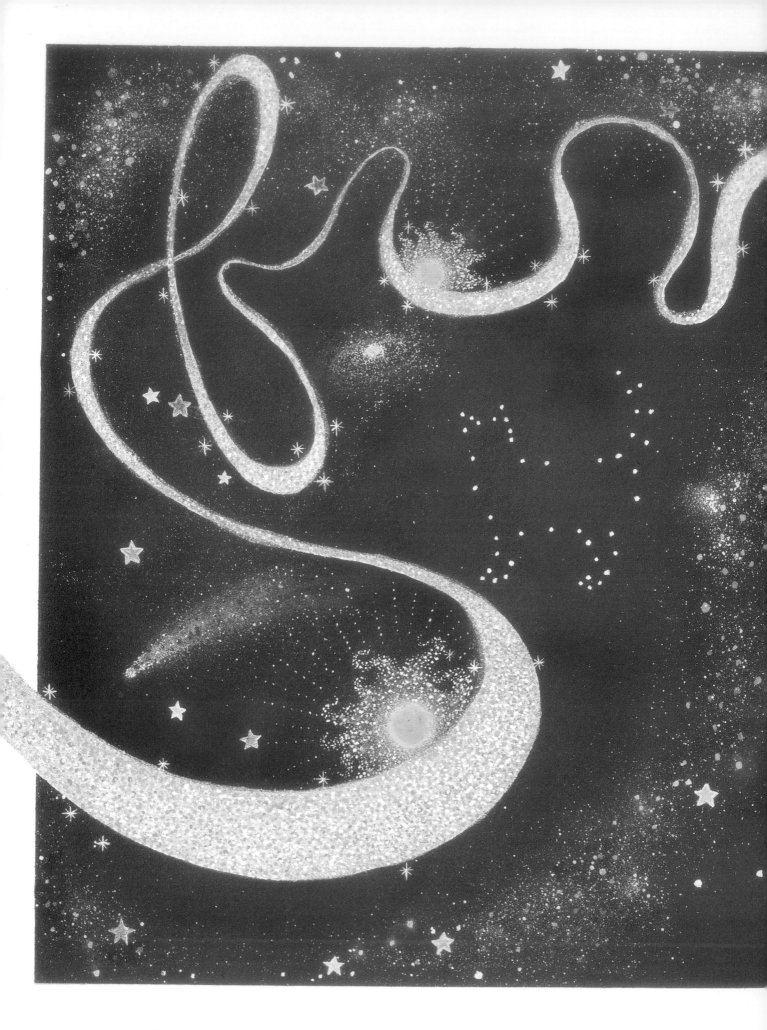

When you open your heart and your fun tumbles out,
News of it travels a heavenly route.
It soars through the galaxies, igniting each sun,
And the stars are ablaze...with your feeling of fun."

CHARA M. CURTIS

Born in Minnesota, Chara has lived in a variety of places, including northern Wisconsin, Nashville, Chicago, and Istanbul. She now makes her home near the San Juan Islands of Washington, where writing is her full-time vocation.

Though her expression takes many forms, Chara enjoys collaboration and the process of integrating visual with verbal images. "As with music," she says, "images lift words into the realm of unutterable emotion and understanding. They add focus to our imagination without limiting the depth of our journeys."

Chara's other published works include two from Illumination Arts, *How Far to Heaven?* and *All I See Is Part of Me*. In 1997, she received a Washington State Governor's Writers Award for *No One Walks on My Father's Moon* from Voyage Publishers.

CYNTHIA ALDRICH

Cynthia was born and raised in the Pacific Northwest. Since graduating from the University of Washington with a major in painting and graphic art, she has traveled a number of creative pathways.

Fun Is A Feeling is Cynthia's second collaboration with author Chara M. Curtis. Their classic children's picture book, *All I See Is Part of Me*, was awarded an inaugural *Body Mind Spirit Magazine* Award of Excellence in 1996. Her works, in a wide variety of media, are displayed in numerous private collections. She currently lives in southeastern Utah.

P.O. Box 1865, Bellevue, WA 98009
888-210-8216 • 425-644-7185
425-644-9274 fax • liteinfo@illumin.com

Library of Congress Cataloging in Publication Data

Curtis, Chara M. 1950–
      Fun is a feeling / words by Chara M. Curtis; illustrations by
      Cynthia Aldrich ; concept by Chara and Cynthia.
          p. cm.
      Summary: A child discovers that the joy of life comes from
      within and that attitude is all-important.
      ISBN 0-935699-13-9 : $15.95
      1. Children's poetry, American. [1. American poetry.]
  I. Aldrich, Cynthia, 1947– . II. Title.
  PS3553.U694F8   1992
  811'.54—dc20

Library of Congress Number 91-41875

Fourth Printing, 2008
Published in the United States of America

Printed by Tien Wah Press in Singapore

Cover Designer:
Peri Poloni, Knockout Design, Naperville, IL

More inspiring picture books from Illumination Arts

God's Promise
Maureen Moss / Gerald Purnell, ISBN 978-0-9740190-7-9
As her family eagerly awaits the birth of their baby girl, God helps Angelina prepare for her life on Earth. This tender story will touch readers of all ages.

Am I a Color Too?
Heidi Cole / Nancy Vogl / Gerald Purnell, ISBN 978-0-9740190-5-5
A young interracial boy wonders why people are labeled by the color of their skin. Seeing that people dream, sing and love regardless of their color, he asks, *Am I a Color Too?*

Roonie B. Moonie: Lost and Alone
Janan Cain, ISBN 978-0-9740190-8-6
Lost in an unfamiliar place, an adventurous young bee must follow his instincts and use his head in order to avoid danger and keep himself safe.

A Mother's Promise
Lisa Humphrey / David Danioth, ISBN 978-0-9701907-9-6
A lifetime of sharing begins with the sacred vow a woman makes to her unborn child – a promise to share the wonders of life, and to love and protect her child to be.

Just Imagine
John Thompson / George Schultz / Wodin, ISBN 978-0-9740190-6-2
Ready for fun and adventure? Who knows what might happen as our imaginations take flight! Anything is possible when we *Just Imagine*.

Mrs. Murphy's Marvelous Mansion
Emma Roberts / Robert Rogalski, ISBN 978-0-9740190-4-8
Mrs. Murphy's snobbish neighbors are convinced that her strange little house should be torn down – until she invites them for lunch and they learn the secret of inner beauty.

The Tree
Dana Lyons / David Danioth, ISBN 978-0-9701907-1-0
An eight-hundred-year-old Douglas fir tree tells of the interconnectedness of all things and sounds an urgent call to preserve our fragile environment.

We Share One World
Jane Hoffelt / Marty Husted, ISBN 978-0-9701907-8-9
Wherever we live – whether we work in the fields, the waterways, the mountains or the cities – all people and creatures share one world.

One Smile
Cindy McKinley / Mary Gregg Byrne, ISBN 978-0-935699-23-4
A girl's innocent smile sparks a chain reaction of kindness that touches an entire community. Children and adults alike will be inspired to pass *One Smile* on to everyone they meet.

To view our whole collection, please visit **www.illumin.com**.

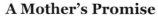